KB178211

A Mother's Hand is
a Healing Hand

A journey to find one's true purpose in life

Ora C

What is the true value of your life?

Ora C

On the top of Haleakala in Maui, Hawaii

___A Mother's Hand is a Healing Hand___

Part 1, Finding the balance in life

Part 2, Transformation

1, Transformation

Part 3, Ora: Come to me

Prologue

      A sudden, mysterious voice, emerging out of nowhere in my homeland of South Korea, called me to journey to America. Compelled by this unseen force, I landed in New York City, the first place where my new life in the U.S. began in 1999. However, after 6 years of immersing myself in the pulse of New York, my journey took an unexpected turn. I became a nomad, drifting through different lives and places.

      The nomadic journey carried me from one place to the next- New York, San Francisco, Los Angeles, and Maui, Hawaii. With each move, I became more attuned to my instincts and intuition. Along the way, I developed a deeper understanding of myself and came to appreciate the diverse ways people live, connecting with individuals from various cultures and backgrounds. This enriched perspective not only broadened my worldview but also gave me the tools to navigate new environments confidently.

      When I set off for my next destination, I packed a suitcase, a backpack, two yoga mats, and a few thousand dollars- my only belongings. Settling a new place was never easy, especially at the beginning. Yet, with each transition, I felt a sense of accomplishment, as if I were earning a trophy.

Throughout the chapters of my life, a sudden profound shift occurred in April 2018 while I was in Los Angeles. It was a powerful calling to *write*. Until then, I had never written for publication, especially not in English. Strangely enough, as soon as I began writing, my life became dramatically more challenging. Yet, instead of shying away from the struggle, I chose to embrace it. I saw these hardships as the raw material for the first chapter of my book, and it continued to explore the beginning of my journey and the process of tuning into my true path.

I hope this book reaches those who feel lost in the direction of their lives, inspiring them to tune into the flow of their own journey and discover their true path.

Ora C

On Market street in San Francisco, 2014

Ora C

Inside Haleakakala crater in Maui, Hawaii, 2015

Kirti Christiana Wright

Kirti Christiana Wright

In 2019, after enrolling in massage school in Maui, Hawaii, I got to know Kirti Christina Wright. Kirti was a fellow student at school. A month after classes began, she planned to leave Maui and return to her home in California (she is originally from Alaska). Before she left Maui, I invited her to have a cup of tea. During our conversation, she said from her heart,

"Ora, I studied English literature in college. I would be happy to help you edit the grammar of your writing if you want. I won't charge you."

I was surprised by her help. I had been searching for an editor within a tight budget for my writing. Her hard work and warmheartedness are much appreciated. Kirti edited my first piece, which I finished in December 2019. Since then, I gained the confidence to continue writing on my own. After more than 7 years of writing, I finally completed and published my book.

Part 1,
Finding the balance in life

1, Finding my frequency

High Frequency

      A group of children held sky-high balloons and ran through the park. Roman, the 7-year-old boy I was babysitting, had started playing with them. Curious, I walked over to see who he was hanging out. It turned out they all were waiting for the birthday party of Roman's friend's sister to begin. It was a peaceful late afternoon at Kihei Park in Maui, Hawaii, during the fall of 2018.

    As I fully immersed myself in the children's joyful energy, I suddenly felt a strong force flowing to me. I turned, searching for the source of this energy, and saw a woman in the distance. She was staring at me with an intense gaze. The moment our eyes met, she began walking toward me. Her name is Irina, and she is originally from Russia. She had recently moved from New York to Maui. She was one of the parents of the kids attending the birthday celebration. We quickly fell into a fascinating conversation, and I said,

"Isn't it interesting? You and I had lived in the same neighborhoods, East Village, and Union Square Park in New York City during the same years. We might have even crossed paths on the same streets, but we never bumped into each other or recognized one another until now. However, after this encounter, we are both aware of our existence. Furthermore, you moved to America in the same year I did, 1999, triple 9! And you were doing modeling in New York City, just like I was. How incredible that we share all these synchronicities!"

She then responded seriously,

"People who resonate the same frequency tend to attract one another. It was as if we were energetically aligned, which allowed us to connect and meet. For example, individuals vibrating at 741 Hz are more likely to cross paths with others who share that frequency, just as those resonating at 963 Hz will. Of course, we meet people with different frequencies all the time, but if they don't match our own, a deep connection may not form. The reason, you and I recognize each other now is because we resonate on the same frequency,"

What she said gave me goosebumps and completely blew

my mind.

"That's so interesting! Then, how can we raise our frequency?" I asked.

She paused for a second to gather her thoughts before responding to my question, and she said,

"With a clear mind, we can increase our frequency."

I put my hands on my head, astonished by her words.

"Oh, my God! What you just said aligns perfectly with my writing, too! It is another synchronicity! I unexpectedly started writing earlier this year, the theme of my work is how we can overcome obstacles in our lives by cultivating a clear mind. After over 20 years in America, I discovered this through meditation, which helped me navigate a nomadic lifestyle in a foreign country." I said.

With a clear mind, we can observe how our thoughts and emotions shift from moment to moment. This awareness allows us to raise our frequency. The higher our frequency, the more we align with greater phenomena and events. This is the power of awareness.

At the moment of Evergreen and Ora
sharing the same frequency in Maui, Hawaii.

Photoed by Julie Christine

Share (Tree of Life)

Just as I was about to take a bite of the strawberry in my car, a man approached me. It was a sunny day, in April 2019 in Pukalani, Maui, Hawaii.

"Hi," he said,

"Hi," I responded, noticing his T-shirt, "Nice shirt, very artistic!"

"Thank you," he smiled. "I designed this, and I am an artist. I also make hip-hop music, too." He responded.

He began telling me more about himself he spent most of his time creating art, not prioritizing physical comfort, often sleeping in his car, and so on. But then, he shared a heartbreaking struggle of not having enough money to bring his 8-year-old child to Maui. After he spoke, the voice in my heart began speaking to him,

"I respect what you do," I said. "However, I believe it is important to maintain a balance between the physical world and the realm of our dream. While we do not need excessive material possessions to survive, we need necessities for our physical bodies, such as food, shelter, and clothing. It is through the physical realm that we learn many life lessons. And especially for children, nurturing is essential. They rely on the love and guidance of their parents to grow and thrive."

I took a moment to catch my breath and noticed that he was listening intently. So, I continued to say,

"I currently work on an organic farm. Twice a week, I plant hundreds of seedlings in the field. Before planting, these baby plants require fertilizer, and once they are in the ground, they need regular watering, weeding, and spraying to protect them from insects. Without this care, they would not thrive or bear fruit. It's much like a tree's needs— sunlight, water, soil, attention, etc. Once the tree reaches maturity, it bears fruit, completing its life cycle. I am not saying you have to give up what you love to do. Keep pursuing your passion whenever you can. And as your kid grows, you'll have more time to devote to your art."

I saw his eyes shining as he took my words.

"Thank you, Ora. Do you drink coconut water?" He appreciated me and handed me one of the canned coconut waters.

A month later, I received a text from him,

"Aloha Ora, this is Kii. We met at the Foodland parking lot. You were telling me about the Tree of Life... I am interested in having a massage session with you."

As I massaged him, I considered offering him a discount, feeling a sense of generosity. After an hour of work,

"How are you feeling? The session is over." I checked in him.

"Oh, are you done already?" he replied. "Can you do it another 30 minutes? I would like to have a 90-minute massage rather than a 60-minute one. I feel better after just an hour" he said.

"I only gave you an hour because I was worried about your financial situation, with you sleeping in your car, and not able to bring your kid here..." I responded.

"Ora, after I met you, I started making good money." He said.

"Really? How?" I asked him.

"I am installing marble countertops in kitchens now. I make $2,500 a week. Now, I am looking for a place. As soon as I find one, I will bring my kid and the mother of the kid on Maui from the mainland." He said.

"Oh, my God, that's fantastic! I am so happy for you!" I responded.

I felt a natural high from his good news that remained long after the conversation ended.

When hearts are open, we resonate with each other. Sharing happiness and joy amplifies those feelings while sharing sorrow helps lighten the burden. We humans are complex beings, with energy constantly flowing through our bodies. In my experience, face-to-face communication allows us to share and resonate with each other's energy more effectively and positively in a way that phone calls cannot. Positive in-person interactions can boost our oxytocin levels, contributing to feelings of happiness and connection rather than loneliness.

Resonating with each other's energy was similar to spreading mycelium among trees to help them in a forest.

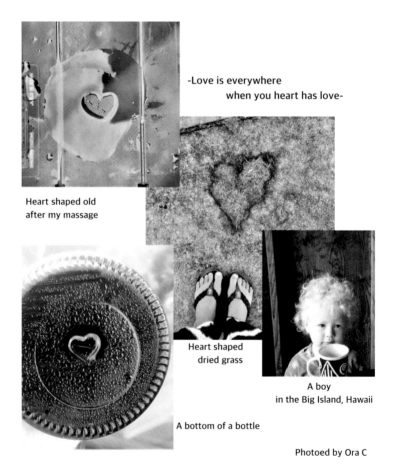

-Love is everywhere
when you heart has love-

Heart shaped old
after my massage

Heart shaped
dried grass

A boy
in the Big Island, Hawaii

A bottom of a bottle

Photoed by Ora C

Gratitude (Branscomebe Richmond)

All the help and offerings I have received during my nomadic life journey are priceless.

'My thumb went up, and then a car would stop.'

Maui's public buses ran infrequently—about once every hour or hour and a half, depending on the route—and they did not cover the entire island. Since I often saw people hitchhiking around the island, and I did not have a car at that time, I decided to give it a try. In 2006, after moving in Maui, I became a hitchhiker for the first time.

Despite some people having negative opinions about hitchhiking, most drivers who picked me up were friendly. Some drivers went out of their way to take me to my destination, even though it was not on their route. Hitchhiking soon became a valuable network as I was a newcomer to the island. Through it, I met people from all over the world, locals,

28

and from Romania, Hungary, Israel, Brazil, Fiji, and more.

One day, Marty, whom I also met while hitchhiking, invited me to a party where he was scheduled to perform. The event was a celebration for the new Maui film commissioner and was set to take place at the commissioner's house in December 2014. However, a few days before the event, Marty had a sudden severe injury, which caused him to cancel his performance. As a result, I had to attend alone. I was staying in Launiupoko, doing the WWOOF program, and needed to hitchhike to Wailea, where the party was held. To get there, I had to catch three different rides.

During the first two rides, I managed to change from my casual clothes into an evening dress in their cars. Thankfully, the drivers did not mind once I explained where I was headed. The third driver took me all the way to the commissioner's house, dropping me off right in front of the property. He passed through the iron gate to enter the property, informed the gatekeeper of my invitation, and the gate swung open. I was truly grateful to all three drivers for their kindness.

The party began, but it was not quite the vibe I expected. After an hour, I was ready to leave. Just as I was about to head out, three tall men walked in. Their entrance was like something out of a movie– the kind where the hero arrived and transformed the atmosphere from dull to electrifying. They were Branscombe Richmond and his two sons. I ended up spending the next few hours with his sons, completely losing track of time at the four–hour party.

As it began to wind down, I began to feel frustrated and anxious. I usually avoid hitchhiking at nighttime. I started to ask the people at the party if anyone was heading in my direction. But instead of offering help, they laughed and pointed out that I had hitchhiked there. Just as my discomfort was building, Branscombe approached me and said,

"Ora, don't worry. I will give you a ride." Branscombe said with a reassuring smile.

"Oh, my God? Thank you so much!" I replied, my voice filled with surprise and gratitude.

What made his offer even more remarkable was the fact that he lived in Kula, a long distance in the opposite direction from Launiupoko.

In Branscombe's car, he was accompanied by his friend and his two tall, handsome sons. The whole situation felt surreal, almost like stepping into a fairy tale. It was as if I were

Cinderella, except instead of the pumpkin turning into the carriage, I had four awesome men guarding me, making me feel like someone truly special. This unexpected event filled me with an exhilarating sense of joy, a natural high that elevated my frequency. And that high frequency lingered for a long time.

If I had the money to buy a car at that time, I would not have had the opportunity to meet such kind and warmhearted people through hitchhiking, nor would I have made wonderful friends so quickly. It felt as though I was creating something out of nothing, much like the universe itself. This experience taught me that, as humans, we have the power to create something meaningful out of a lack of resources.

Hitchhiking was once one of the most beautiful cultures on Maui. However, in 2022, hitchhikers had become rare, and finding a ride had grown difficult. Because many of the people who used to offer me rides had moved away, and new people had taken their place. It calls, "gentrification."

At Dragon Fruit Farm
in Launiupoko, Maui,
2014

Photoed by Ora C

Branscombe Richmond & Ora
on the left,
& Branscomebes, his sons, me
and his friend below

Photoed by Penny Palmer
& Kim Sloan

Breathing

Deep inhalations and exhalations can help clear our minds of fear and anxiety.

"Ora never made a mistake!" my co-worker teased me while working.

It was as busy and chaotic as any other day at work. Some employees dropped food while serving, and others suddenly screamed. It was at the restaurant where I began to work in San Francisco, in December 2015.

As soon as I arrived in San Francisco from Maui, Hawaii, I started to apply for a job. I found a hiring and sent them my resume. They responded with the interview schedule on the same day I emailed them. And during the interview, they hired me as a server. The restaurant from the Japanese corporation company was preparing to open as the first location in America.

Soon after its opening, it quickly became popular within a few months. However, to improve the restaurant system, the managers and leaders constantly changed daily rules, confusing employees. In addition, the intense pressure of working five hours without a break led many workers to make mistakes. They dropped food, and in their frustration, screamed during shifts. The stress was overwhelming, and exhaustion left me feeling miserable. I cried every night before falling asleep. Then, one night, I prayed deeply,

'Please help me to survive this hell!' After the prayer, something shifted the following day.

It started like any other chaotic day. However, as I worked at my usual pace, I began to see the entire restaurant—how it ran and operated. With each step I took, I started breathing deeply, and with each breath, my mind cleared like the blue sky. With that clarity, I was able to assist my coworkers while staying focused on my tasks. Whenever they needed a hand, even before they asked me, I helped them. I also managed customers' seating arrangements and ensured clear communication between the front and the back of the house. Additionally, I handled customer complaints with care. Sometimes, I shared jokes with the customers, and both they and I laughed heartily, leading to generous tips. Eventually, I became the team's leader on many occasions.

Through deep breathing, a stressful situation turned into five hours of exciting playtime and saved my life.

With clarity, we can perceive more of the world around us. It helps us navigate life more effectively and raises our frequency.

San Francisco streets 2016-2017

Photoed by Ora C

−Creative or loving or caring thoughts invoke high frequency emotions, such as appreciation, forgiveness, and joy, and raise the frequency of your system... high frequency will soothe, or calm, or refresh you because of the effect of the quality of its Light upon your system. Such a system is "radiant."−

In the Book, 'The Seat of the Soul' by Gary Zukav

2, Balance

I have lived by my heart-pounding intuition.

Steve Jobs said this: Have the courage to follow your heart and intuition. They somehow already know what you truly want to become. Everything else is secondary.

'Think different...-Steve Jobs-'

'All the strange pieces came together to create this beautiful image...as humans, so can we
-Michael Jackson'

On the street in Venice, Los Angeles, 2018
Photoed by Ora C

Writing 1 (Living in balance)

During ten years of dedicating my practices to spiritual awakening and numerous travels, I did not prioritize establishing external conditions.

In the spring of 2018, as purple flowers bloomed across Los Angeles, I had a realization. It was that, while I have this physical form, I could continue to reach a deeper level of awakening. Then, a question arose. After several weeks of pondering the question, I approached Paul Park, a Zen guiding teacher at the Dharma Zen Center in L.A.

"How can I balance between the physical and the spiritual realms?" I asked.

"Do 500 full prostration bows per day for 100 days," he said right away.

I immediately understood what he meant and began practicing the 500 bows. The first and second days of practice were challenging but my body adapted by the third day.

The more I practiced, my unconscious habitual mind and old karma became clearer. In this process, my actions and words evolved to be more appropriate. As a result, I was able to have a good relationship with the people around me. Then, a month after the bowing practice, a new passion was born: *writing*. I have never written a book, particularly in English. While I was overjoyed with my newfound love of writing, the universe put me to a test.

I have been using massage to heal people since moving to Los Angeles in 2017. However, the website where people could find my healing work vanished unexpectedly. It meant I had to get another job to pay my bills. Strangely, after two months of searching, no one had responded to me for an interview. Eventually, I decided to leave the Zen center, where I had been both practicing and residing, and move to San Francisco to stay with my friend. I believed that I could finish my writing and practice 500 bows within a month without worrying about the finances. Thankfully, my friend offered me a place to stay. As I was preparing to leave, a Zen practitioner came to the center. She said to me after hearing about my situation.

"Writing is the rich people's thing. If you don't have enough money to pay your rent, you should get a job instead of writing."

Regardless, of her advice, I did not change my mind; I had already done everything I could to find work, so I left for San Francisco.

Two days after arriving in Golden Gate City, I encountered unexpected roadblocks. It was at the end of April 2018. Firstly, I dropped the computer by accident, and it completely disintegrated. Secondly, a week after I arrived, my friend, with whom I was staying, informed me that his new girlfriend would be moving in a few weeks. They would soon need the room where I was staying. It was a frustrating situation, but I had no time to get emotional. So, I began to focus on finding the solution.

First, day in and day out, for 10 days of searching for a new computer, I found one. It was not brand new but was a cleaner, lighter, and more recent version than the broken one. The next mission was to transfer the data from the dead computer to the new one. At that time, I had less than $3,000. So, instead of paying $100 to hire a technician, I decided to try it myself. I held the new computer on my chest and pondered the question, walking through downtown San Francisco. When I arrived at Union Square Park, I sat on the cement stairs, placed my new computer on my lap, and closed my eyes. Then, I took a deep breath and focused on the question,

'How can I transfer the data?'

About 30 minutes passed, and a man flashed across my mind like a lightning bolt. He was employed at Apple in Silicon Valley. I immediately texted him with the question, and he responded with a simple direction.

'There is a way!'

As soon as I resolved the computer issue, I began to run around the city, looking for a job and a place to live in San Francisco, while continuing to practice 500 bows.

Writing 2 (Following the next journey)

It was the 98th day of my 500-bow practice. I boarded a local bus, feeling restlessness in both body and mind from my search for a place to stay and a job in San Francisco. The bus came to a stop at 14 Street in the Mission district.

At that moment, the ray of the setting sun pierced through the gap between the edge of the thick fog and the summit of a hill, streaming into the bus where I sat. It was an incredible, bright, golden beam of light that I felt deeply it penetrated my heart. Then, I spontaneously prayed,

'Please show me a sign where to go, where I can complete my writing, and where my next destination is?'

Just as I finished praying, the bus ran again and stopped at the next stop. Suddenly, my eyes widened at what I saw, threatening and overwhelming me like crashing ocean waves: 'Oh, my God! No, no, no, no⋯'.

There was a van parked at the bus stop with a sticker on its back window that read *Maui*.

It was 100 consecutive days of bowing practice when I decided to return to the Zen Center. Thankfully, the shanga (Buddhist community) welcomed me back, allowing me to take some time before finding my next destination. However, the strange things occurred after returning to L.A. I kept seeing, 'Maui', 'Aloha', and 'Hawaii' signs wherever I went. It caused a constant internal conflict within my mind: *'Yes, you gotta go to Maui', 'No, I don't want to', 'Yes', 'No', 'Yes', 'No'.*

After a few weeks of inner turmoil, I jumped on a bus to go to Venice Beach to clear my mind.

While sitting on the vast, white, sandy beach and gazing at the blue ocean soothed my spirit and helped me to relax. Then, I closed my eyes and meditated. A sensation in my gut emerged as if a seed were sprouting. Going to Maui was no longer just a dream—it was becoming a reality. And I felt that this journey would present more challenges than any I had before. Nonetheless, I no longer resisted knowing where the next destination would be. So, I began to consider where I would work and live. Then, a woman appeared in my mind, someone who owned a high-end jewelry studio. I had known her since

I first moved to Maui in 2006.

"Are you coming back?" she asked me.

To my surprise, she texted me back immediately after I texted her.

"Yes, I was wondering if you need a helper for your studio," I replied, asking her for a job.

She told me she was looking for a helper. The timing could not have been more perfect! After our conversation, I contacted the previous farm owner, where I used to take a WWOOF program. She expressed her welcome for my return. Everything seemed perfectly aligned with my plan: I could live and work on the farm five days a week while earning some money at the jewelry studio for two days.

Though these two places were set, I was not entirely confident about what the future would hold. Yet, I decided to go to Maui. I booked a one-way flight and left for Maui sometime in June 2018.

in Miracle Miles, L.A, 2018

In Mission District, San Francisco, 2018   Photoed by Ora C

The initiation of living on Maui

It had not been long since I arrived on Maui when I was given two days of the trial for two weeks. Despite my expectations, the jewelry studio owner did not teach me how to sell her jewelry during the trial. Due to my no prior experience in this field, particularly with high‑end jewelry, I was not hired. Instead of feeling disappointed, I appreciated her. As the job required a car, I found one within 10 days.

Meanwhile, during two weeks of trials, the farm where I intended to participate in the WWOOF program filled its positions with other applicants. It was a busy season that they needed workers right away. Neither the jewelry studio nor the farm worked out as I anticipated. While dealing with this situation, the car I purchased for $900 started to indicate trouble. It was a few days after I bought a car. I was driving down the Hana Highway in Haiku around 7 p.m.

Suddenly, my car made a loud noise and tipped to the right side. I quickly pulled over my car, realizing that the passenger side of the tire had completely blown out and was beyond repair. The road where I had stopped had tiny shoulders, and a guardrail prevented me from moving any further down. This caused traffic congestion on the highway. I panicked because I did not have any towing company's number or had any assistance for the moment. I climbed back into my car and desperately prayed for,

'Please, help.'

Shortly after my prayer, a car pulled over in front of my car. And a woman got off her car, and said,

"Are you ok?" she asked me.

'Thank God! Someone stopped to help me!' I spoke inside. I stepped out of my car and looked at her. Tears started welling up in my eyes,

"I don't know what happened to my car. I just got this car three days ago. And I just moved back to Maui..." I explained feeling overwhelmed.

Just then, another car pulled over, and a man got off his

car, and asked,

"Are you ok?"

As soon as he figured out my car situation, he helped move it to the other side of the road, into a grassy area where I could leave my car overnight. The woman who had stopped for me kindly offered me a ride to my lodging. I was deeply grateful to Caron and Kevin for their help that night.

The following day, TD, a new friend on Maui, assisted me change the spare tire. I then took it to the tire shop, only to find out that I needed to replace all four tires with brand-new ones. This left me nearly empty in my pocket, and I could not help but I felt fear about my situation.

It was nearly 10 p.m. I calmed myself and faced my reality. With no other option that night, I decided to sleep in my car, even though sleeping in a car was scary. I drove around, searching for a safe spot for the night. Eventually, I found one and stopped. I rolled down the window and reclined the seat. As I breathed deeply, I gazed at the countless stars. In that moment, I prayed to them,

'Please, help me get through this situation. Help me to find

some private yoga students or massage clients.'

During my prayer, I saw a glimpse of a man in my closed-eyed visions and fell asleep.

Praying Ora
At FS hotel in Maui, Hawaii , 2018

Meeting Dr. Ryan

It had been ten days since I had slept in my car, and I was nearly losing my mind from the situation. Then, suddenly, I heard a voice say, "*Go to the beach!*" I followed the voice and turned toward Baldwin Beach.

I walked aimlessly along the beach for a while. Suddenly, the sound of crashing waves reached my ears, and my mind returned to the present moment after I saw a man in the distance. He looked the same man I had seen with my eyes closed while praying on the first night I slept in my car. I began walking closer to him, breathing rapidly due to surprise.

As I passed, one of his playful dogs began following me.

Obvious of everything else except the dog, I tripped over a rock, not paying attention to my path. The man, now known as Dr. Ryan, rushed over to me, and apologized,

"Are you ok? Sorry about my dog. Ninja, come here,"

In fact, the distraction from Ninja became a bridge for us to have a conversation.

Dr. Ryan was preparing to compete in the World Master Swimming Championship, which explained why he was wearing a black, tight, mini swimming suit on the beach. It was not a typical bathing suit for men on the beach on Maui. I briefly wondered, 'Is he European?' After he introduced himself, I shared where I was from and told him about Kouk Sun Do, a Korean healing yoga I teach. Without hesitation, he immediately asked me,

"Could you be my private yoga teacher, please?"

"Oh, okay! Can I have your number then? I will contact you when I have a chance." I responded.

I almost jumped up off the ground into the air, filled with excitement by my manifestation. His words made me so excited that sounded like a blur of, 'Ooh, ooh, ooh, ooh...' while he continued talking. As our conversation was winding down, he said,

"I don't swim to compare. I just enjoy challenging myself to improve and become faster."

He was one of the most inspirational people in my life. His daily routine consisted of swimming at 5 a.m. every morning. After swimming, he worked out at the gym every other day. Then he began to work at 9 a.m. and finished at 6 p.m. While he was my yoga student, he competed in two championships—one in Malaysia and the other in Australia—and won a gold medal for each. He sent me a text from each country,

"Thank you very much, Ora. Your teaching and yoga contributed greatly to the outcome,"

Shortly after meeting Dr. Ryan, I no longer had to sleep in the car. I was offered a part-time live-in nanny job in exchange for a work trade. It was a perfect deal at that time. This is how my journey began on Maui in 2018.

Teaching Dr. Ryan Kouk Sun Do in 2018

Photoed by Ora C

3, Inner freedom

Spontaneous healing

Mira who was a makeup artist and hairdresser invited me to join her to work at the Marriott resort in Wailea. It was in August 2018. While she was working, I had a chance to spend my time at Wailea Beach.

Strangely, Mira had not called me even after a couple of hours had passed from her work. Rather than just waiting, I decided to call her.

"Ora, hurry and come upstairs!" she said.

When I opened the door of the room, I saw Mira supporting her assistant, who was lying on the floor. I rushed over to her and checked her body. Her body was cold as ice and hard as a rock. In that critical moment, I thought to myself, *'She is in danger. We need to call 911'.* But another thought quickly came to my mind, *'If I just waited for the ambulance without doing anything, it might be too late to save her'.* So, I just began massaging her with the one thought:

'Save her.'

After a while of massaging her, she began to move slowly Mira, and I helped her in her car and drove her home. While driving, I realized I had been massaging her non-stop for over an hour.

Two days later, I received a text message from Mira's assistant. She expressed her gratitude for saving her life and stated that her condition had stabilized. And the next day, she mentioned that she had also received acupuncture treatments. Surprisingly, within a few days, her condition returned to normal. This incident reminded me of my mother's healing touch.

When I was a little girl, my mother used to rub the troublesome spot on my body while repeating a mantra,

"A Mother's Hand Healing is a Healing hand, a mother's hand is a healing hand (in Korean, 'Umma Soni Yaksonida')..."

By her magical touch and the mantra relived the pain in my body.

At the end of massaging Mira's assistant in 2018

Photoed by Ora C

Resilience 1 (Self-Healing)

After teaching Kouk Sun Do, becoming a nanny, and then, working as a farmer in an organic farm, I found that deep inside, my desire to obtain a Hawaiian massage license was growing stronger. It was in September 2019.

To earn the license, I needed to attend massage school. However, my income from farm work was insufficient to cover Maui's high rent and school tuition. Eventually, I gave up my room, deciding to sleep in a tent and attend the class. Just a few days after sleeping in a tent, something dramatic happened.

In the morning, I noticed water inside the tent from the previous night's heavy rainfall. As I stood up, I was in excruciating pain in my left upper body— my neck, trapeze, and arm. The level of pain was so intense that I had to stop my car several times a day. Despite my difficult physical condition, I continued to go to work and attend school. After suffering from the pain for 1 month, I finally went to see a doctor.

The doctor suggested that I take some painkillers. However, I chose not to, as I had developed sensitivities and allergies to Western medications. This sensitivity had developed as a result of not taking Western medication for two decades, especially since I did not have health insurance in America. Over time, I started to feel overwhelmed by my situation, so I decided to drop out of school.

When I explained my circumstance to the school's coordinator, the wife of the director, she gave me an option,

"Why don't you work for school instead of dropping out? You can clean the school before it opens, and we can deduct the tuition from your working hours. And you can also pay the rest of the tuition when you are ready to pay." She said.

Instead of thinking impossible, her suggestion touched my heart and made me cry. The following day, I started cleaning the school.

I woke up at 4:30 a.m. and went to school at 5 a.m. After 2 hours cleaning school, I started working at the farm at 7:30 a.m. and finished at 1 or 2 p.m. After farming, I had to prepare to attend a class at the school from 5 p.m. to 9 p.m. And I realized again,

'*With a strong will, we humans can overcome physical obstacles.*'

Meanwhile, I found a room and began healing my body in my way.

First, I swam in the ocean for about an hour, 2 or 3 times a week, hoping to wash away the mysterious pain in my body.

Secondly, despite the pain, I stretched the left side every day.

Thirdly, I massaged myself even in hard-to-reach areas.

Finally, I meditated and prayed to clear any negative energies that could be causing pain in my body. After two months of dedicated self-healing, the pain was significantly reduced. Four months later, I was fully recovered. It felt like I had received a newborn body. One of the teachers in massage school who had seen my endurance said,

"Ora, you are a warrior!"

After completing my self-healing journey, everything seemed peaceful for a few months. Then, the universe threw me another test.

As driving, I suddenly started sneezing uncontrollably.

I had to pull over and take some raw garlic. It was sometime in April of 2020.

For a few years, I had developed the habit of carrying raw garlic with me. I discovered that a few raw garlic cloves could prevent illness from the first sign of a bad sneeze or a chill. However, even after consuming 5 or 6 raw garlic cloves this time, I still felt a persistent chill. Panic began to set in as I realized the symptoms aligned with the ongoing pandemic it was in the early stages of COVID-19. To calm myself, I took a deep breath. With faith of surviving, I drove home to prepare the natural remedies that would help fight off the illness.

Firstly, I made a special hot tea. I chopped fresh raw ginger and boiled it in a pot of water. After pouring the hot ginger brew into a cup, I added ginseng, turmeric, and cinnamon powders, and the juice of a whole fresh lemon. This tea warmed my body up while also providing a vitamin C boost. I drank this tea regularly throughout my illness.

Next, I made a free-range organic chicken soup with vegetables, lots of hot chili peppers, and plenty of garlic and ginger. The soup made me sweat a lot, clearing my sinuses and lungs. And the chicken provided me with a good source of protein. Interestingly, during this illness, my body craved beans. So, I cooked and ate some. Later, I discovered that beans are rich in essential minerals.

Third, I went to the park, dressed in multiple layers to sweat more and ran up and down the stairs for about 30 minutes.

Lastly, I slept all day except for work, giving my white blood cells needed rest from their constant battle with the virus. After 8 days of illness, I completely recovered. And then, a miracle happened.

Throughout my life, I used to catch a cold a couple of times a month. During those times, I would lie in bed, completely out of it for a few days. However, since that eight-day illness, I have not been sick at all for the past two years-until now. I also no longer take raw garlic every day, as my immune system significantly improved during those 8 days of sickness!

The more interesting thing was that just three days before I fell ill, Dr Michael Lee (J.H. Lee), an oriental in New Jersey, contacted me to share his methods for treating C-19. The timing was perfect, and his guidance provided to be a great inspiration for my healing. I truly appreciated his support.

Soon after recovering, I returned to school, and the clinic

began. Since then, I have been massaging for 4 hours in the clinic and working at the farm for 6 hours a day.

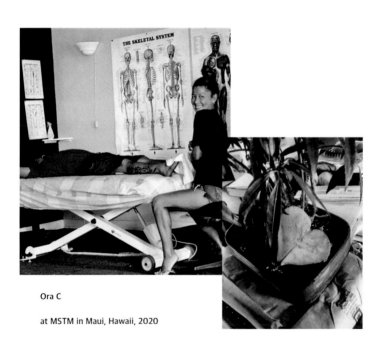

Ora C

at MSTM in Maui, Hawaii, 2020

Resilience 2 <small>(Belief)</small>

Working physically 10 hours a day, both on the farm and at the clinic, pushed my body to its limit. I began to experience numbness, tingling, and weakness in my hands and arms, causing me to frequently drop things.

When I visited the Dr, he diagnosed me with Carpal Tunnel Syndrome (CTS). It was a depressing time, as I could not earn an income or seek any assistance. I had to stop attending school and working on the farm to prevent the condition from worsening. During this difficult period, one question consumed my mind,

'How can I heal my Carpal Tunnel Syndrome?'

About a month after my CTS diagnosis, on August 24th, 2020, I reviewed the anatomy. I carefully palpated my arm's ligaments and muscles. Then I discovered that the Flexor Carpi Radialis muscle and medial elbow were triggering the pain in my wrists. Once I identified the problem, I began massaging those muscles and resting.

After two months of self-healing, my arms and hands significantly improved, allowing me to return to the clinic and start massaging for 16 hours a week. However, due to the pandemic, I could not return to the farm. Shortly after I went back to school, final exam and graduation approaching in November 2020.

Preparing for the exam was a critical challenge. I overloaded my brain with anatomy, physiology, kinesiology, neuromuscular therapy, the laws, and other subjects all day. This intensity of my studying caused me to pass out a couple of times a day, something I had never experienced before. As a result, I passed the exam and attended my graduation ceremony on the same day.

Everyone in the class except me received their diploma. I had failed to complete the required clinic hours and had not paid the full tuition, so I did not receive my diploma. After graduation, I lost faith in myself and became negative about everything. Then, the universe presented me with a major test.

A few weeks after graduation, I was involved in a severe car accident and disposed of my car as a result. The most stressful part was that, regardless of the severity, neither the other party's car insurance nor my insurance company covered the damage. On top of that, I had to endure mental challenges (post-traumatic stress disorder), physical pain (whiplash), and emotional distress (due to dealing with the car insurance company).

However, throughout this extremely difficult situation, my negative mindset completely faded. I began to focus on my daily responsibilities fully and started to believe in myself,

'I can go through this digester and pay off the rest of my tuition one day'.

I returned to school to complete the clinic hours, and thankfully, people I knew who had heard of my accident started offering their help. My landlord kindly offered me rides in emergencies, whether I needed to go to town early in the morning or be picked up from school at night. Additionally, my previous farm owner gave me some donations, and someone I knew delivered me kimchi. I truly appreciate their help. Then, a miracle came my way.

Resilience 3

Diana, whom I met six years ago while participating in the WWOOF program at a farm in 2015, came to visit her friend–my co–worker–for a week. Interestingly, we quickly became friends, and I shared my food and took her to the beach. Since then, I have not seen her in 6 years.

When Diana returned to Maui during the pandemic, and relief funds were starting to be distributed. She helped me to apply for Pandemic Unemployment Assistance (PUA), and shortly after, I was approved. With the PUA, I was able to pay off both my car accident expenses and my school tuition. With my school diploma in hand, I became eligible to take the Hawaiian massage license exam. In March 2021, I become a Hawaiian–licensed massage therapist. It felt like a miracle from God! Along the way, the universe conspired to bring me another reward.

After the accident, I began to take four different buses to work at a spa in Wailea, as I no longer had a car. The commute took five hours round-trip. Instead of buying a car, I hoped to rent one with a small budget. Then, C—whom I had known for 10 years but had not seen in three or four years—contacted me about her physical issues revealed in her MRI. I began treating her based on her symptoms.

Two months after starting treatment, her symptoms improved significantly. She then wanted to continue regular sessions and proposed to me a trade: she would let me use one of her cars in exchange for my 90-minute treatment once a week. I couldn't believe it— my manifestation came true!

Once I started driving her car, people I knew began to notice and comment on it,

"Nice car!"

"It's not mine," I replied with a smile.

Overcoming the stormy period during my year at school was one of the greatest challenges I have ever faced. Once it was over, I saw Lama Gyaltsen and said,

"Lama, I've never felt completely at peace in my life before!"

"Ora, you've gotten enlightened!" He responded with a smile.

Curriculum of the Massage Therapist

Accidental selfie

Photoed by Ora C

A new version of myself

-Overcoming challenge gives a feeling of
an absolute joy like a tree budding
in the early spring after enduring a long winter-

A magnolia tree

photoed by Ora C

As soon as I got my car, I began working at the spa
in a luxury hotel in Wailea. It felt like a new chapter, but soon
after, I found myself facing challenges I had never experienced
before in my career. It was May 2022, in Maui, Hawaii.

During this difficult time, some warmhearted co-workers
and employees from other departments offered me an Aloha
hug.

*A genuine hug from someone who truly cares brings both
courage and healing energy.*

To stay grounded during these tough times, I meditated and prayed days and nights. With all my efforts and resilience, I eventually found a way to break through that barrier I had been facing. Another powerful source of strength came from the positive feedback from the hotel guests who experienced my massage.

Many of them asked for requestion of my treatment, and shared their appreciation with words that stayed with me:

"My pain reduced, " or "It was so relaxing!"

Knowing that, even in the toughest times, my efforts were making a positive impact on others' lives. And hearing their reactions to my massages was the true reward of my work—a deep sense of fulfillment.

I realized that the struggles and challenges I faced in life were not misfortunate. In fact, they were transformative moments that helped me to evolve from an old version of myself into a new one.

The person I once was defined by traits such as a strong ego, hatred, jealousy, attachment, greed, fear, or anger. I came to realize these tendencies did not serve my life well. Yet, through the transitions, I gradually developed the ability to

control them. This, I came to understand, is what 'awareness' truly means.

The more I learned to control these tendencies, the deeper my connection to genuine, heartfelt emotions became, allowing me to live more authentically. Authenticity, in turn, helped me cultivate a strong inner one that was stable and adaptable to the changing conditions around me. Which, I began to experience a sense of inner peace, abundance, and freedom rather than fear and anxiety. It felt like the transformation of a caterpillar into a butterfly.

A caterpillar crawls along the surface. It experiences life with the limitations of its crawling dimension. However, it has the potential to evolve into something greater, a higher being. Before it can soar, the caterpillar must first undergo the pupa stage—the process of metamorphosis, which can be challenging. Within the safety of its cocoon, it endures days or even months of isolation to go through under various weather conditions. After this period of metamorphosis, eventually, it sheds its old karma, emerging completely a new being—the butterfly. No longer a caterpillar, it takes flight freely in a new dimension with wings, carrying it to a height it had never known.

Sky diving Ora,
In Oahu, Hawaii,
2002

'Butterfly'
Selfie

Photoed by Ora C

Part 2,

Transformation

'The world is a book, and those who do not travel read only one page'.

-Saint Augustine-

1, Transformation

Thunder-voice

People who live by following a gut feeling or intuition may face loneliness and challenges. However, trusting these true feelings will guide you onto the right path.

My high school years in South Korea, from the late 1980s to the early 1990s, did not begin smoothly.

We, the students, had to sit in a chair in class all day, taking various exams for every subject. It spanned three years. This program was designed to prepare us for a one-day written exam required for university admission. I tried to follow the program, but after my freshman year, I had reached my limit. I started sleeping in classes instead. As a result, some teachers called me to the teachers' office.

Teachers in South Korea used to hit students with a thick stick, and the size of the stick depended on the teacher's personality. Students who scored lower on a daily exam or displayed an attitude like mine were punished in this way. This led me to lose hope in school life. However, the universe seemed to step in when my school began offering extracurricular activities that included singing, dancing, and acting competitions. These activities transformed my hopeless into great fun. I started to perform in front of over 1,000 students. During each performance, my mind shifted into a state of freedom. In those competitions, I not only won some prizes but also gained many fans. It was the most memorable period of my teen years.

Time flew by, and graduation came. Afterward, all I was left with was loneliness. A year of wandering passed before I finally decided it was time to make money. My first job was as a salesperson at a clothing shop.

The job was not difficult, as I was passionate to fashion at that time. When business was slow, I put some clothes on mannequins in a show window and decorated around them to make the display more appealing. One day, a crowd gathered outside the shop. They entered the shop and asked me,

"I'd like to buy the clothes on that mannequin. Where are they? By the way, who displayed the show window?"

The clothes I dressed the mannequins in sold out, just like the ones I tried on myself in the shop.

'Working with true passion and being fully in the present moment tap into the infinite resources of the universe.'

However, my passion for fashion and working at the clothing store did not last long. It faded dramatically after 3 years. I quit without any concrete plans. My sudden quit upset the shop owner at first, but she later asked me to return, offering better pay. I declined. Since then, I have been taking various temporary jobs here and there, hoping to find one that would reignite my passion again.

In reality, with only a high school diploma, I found no opportunities in Korean society. I began to feel disillusioned with myself and the world I belonged to. This led me down a dark path of self−destruction, numbing my feelings with alcohol and cigarettes day and night. It was a time when I felt completely disconnected from my soul.

For several years, my inner compass was completely off, and suddenly something incredible happened.

I was unconsciously walking down a street. Suddenly, a thunderous voice boomed out of nowhere, and said,

"*Miguk Uro Ga*" (which means '*Go to America*' in Korean).

Since hearing the mysterious voice, I could not think of anything else but going to America. Eventually, I bought a ticket in the summer of 1999.

'Thunder & Fire Om' Collage art

Artist: Ora C

Becoming a model and actress

Following the thunderous voice, I arrived at JFK International Airport in New York in the summer of 1999. The moment I stepped onto the streets of Manhattan, I felt a strong vibration in my gut, and realized,

'This is my place.' My heart felt I had found where I truly belonged.

A few months after enrolling in English classes, I met a remarkable person from somewhere in Africa.

During an insightful conversation with him, he pointed out my judgmental and fixed mindset, which had been deeply influenced by Korean culture. Understanding how my mind had been shaped allowed me to break free from that prison and begin to open my mind. I then integrated into the diverse melting pot, becoming a New Yorker. As I immersed myself in the vibrant city of New York for a couple of years, the longing for a working visa grew strongly.

One day, a poster for the movie, *Chicago* on Manhattan

Street caught my attention.

As the film played, my heart raced, and my gut vibrated fiercely in the middle of the film, '*That's what I want! I want to perform in front of people like Renee Zellweger!*

Following that feeling, I transferred from college to acting class and enrolled at the HB Studio in the West Village, New York.

On the first day of acting classes, I felt so euphoric that I could barely remember how I managed everything. It felt as if I were a fish finally entering the water, where it could breathe and thrive. Just one week after starting school, I discovered an audition for Asian female extras for the movie, '*Memoirs of a Geisha*', directed by Steven Spielberg. Everything seemed to be coming together quickly and seamlessly.

On the day of the audition, I walked into the large hall. Casting calls were posted everywhere—JC Penney, Macy's, and more. I located the line for the 'Memories of Geisha' interview.
When my turn came, I stepped up to a man seated behind a desk. With a stoic expression, he looked me over and asked me a single question,

"Your headshot and resume?"

My brain scrambled to find a response to his request for a second,

"Um, I didn't bring them," I replied with an awkward smile.

"Next!" He immediately rejected me.

For a moment, my mind went blank after his refusal. It was a good lesson that taught me how this industry works. As I regained my mind, I began to walk around the hall. Then a woman behind a desk called me out,

"Excuse me, excuse me! Are you a model?"

"No," I responded to her.

"You are so beautiful! Don't you wanna be a model?" she asked me.

"Yeah" I responded without believing what I had just told.

"Here, call this agent's number", she handed me a modeling agent's number.

"Thank you so much," I replied, still in disbelief at what had just happened to me.

With a mix of excitement and nervousness, I made my way to the agent's office the following day. However, the office turned out to be smaller than I imagined. During my meeting with the agent, a photographer entered the room. After the meeting ended, I stepped out of the room. To catch my breath, I sat on the chair in the hallway. The photographer I had seen earlier walked as well. He sat down beside me and started asking me various questions to figure me out. Once he was done, he asked me,

"Don't you want to have an agency where they can be a sponsor for your working visa?"

I looked at him with big eyes and my thoughts were racing,

'*What? Are you kidding me? That's all I want now!*' The thought raced through my mind, but instead of saying it out loud, I responded,

"Yes, I do."

Two months later, at the age of 31, I became a model and actress, represented by the agency, and was granted a working visa. In that moment of manifesting my dream, I felt like I had everything I could ever want.

The first casting call from the agency was for a background scene in the music video featuring Britney Spears and Madonna. Over 5,000 people came to the casting call, but only 50 people, including me, were selected for it. It felt like everything was off to a good start. Shortly after, I landed another remarkable casting: a commercial for a Nokia phone.

Approximately, 1,000 Asian girls attended the casting call for that commercial. However, the casting team selected only one Asian female, and I was the one chosen. It thrilled me to be selected out of 999 other girls and was paid the most among other modeling gigs.

In the early fall of 2005, my work as Baby Phat print model was featured in prestigious magazines such as Vogue, Elle, Marie Claire, etc. I also landed roles in a music video, an independent film, and some feature films, among others for taking extra roles. Through it all, I was able to channel my passion for expressing myself fully in front of the camera. As my modeling and acting career gained momentum, I received numerous invitations to parties in New York City and became more immersed in the sleepless New York lifestyle. However, as exciting as it all, this lifestyle did not last long.

At a short film, 'Milieu' in New York City, 2005

At Baby Phat shot in New York City, 2005

What is the true purpose of human life?

Two years into my modeling career, the number of castings for Asian models and actresses dropped dramatically, which severely impacted my financial stability. Everything seemed to be falling apart. Having come to the U.S. alone, without family here, I soon found myself isolated−without true friends, a boyfriend, or any job left in a foreign country. The feeling of being lost and uncertain about my life direction in life was overcoming.

It was a gray day in December 2005. The sky above Midtown, New York City, was completely covered by clouds. I made my way up to the rooftop of the building. All I could see was the gray rooftop of the buildings under the gray sky. At that moment, a strange sense of isolation washed over me as I stood there alone, like a character in a movie scene set in an abandoned building in an urban jungle. Then, a strong wind blew by me, '*Shoooh*,' At that moment, a question inside of me arose,

'Why am I here all alone? What am I doing now? What is this?

It was a moment of awe, like a fear of the unknown *'Now'.* For the first time, I felt fully aware of the present moment.

The next day, I was walking down 6th Ave, right by Bryant Park near Times Square. It was at 5 p.m., the peak of rush hour. Suddenly, massive crowds started pouring out of the buildings and merging into the streets. It looked like an enormous ant colony, all moving in the same direction. They walked quickly, and their heads down, toward the subway station. Contradictory, I walked slowly in the opposite direction of the crowd. Despite their hurried pace and head down, no one bumped into me. Instead, it felt as though the path parted with each step I took as if the roads itself were clearing for me. At that moment, another question arose,

' What is the true purpose of human life?'

Carrying these questions in my mind and feeling alone in New York City, I met a remarkable person. It was a night like any other. I was aimlessly walking the streets of Manhattan, then a woman approached me and suddenly stopped

"Excuse me," she called me out. I turned to look at her, awaiting her next words.

"You need to do meditation." She said simply.

Meditation? I thought, confused. "Do I need to do meditation? What is meditation?" I asked, not even knowing what it was at that time.

"You sit and breathe deeply, in and out, for as long as you can," she explained, then turned and walked away.

I had no idea who she was or what her name was. However, this seemingly random encounter–meditation instruction–became a significant turning point in my life. Shortly after meeting her, I felt an undeniable pull toward San Francisco. I wrapped up my six-year stay in New York and made a decision to leave for the West Coast.

Ora at Midtown in New York, 2005

First Meditation

While aimlessly walking down Lower Haight Street,
I prayed desperately,

"Please show me the way. Where should I go?"

It was January 2006, when I left my one-week temporary
accommodation in San Francisco. I had nowhere to go in a
new city, and fear began to rise in me, not knowing where to
go.

After my prayer, I kept walking, trying to push through
uncertainty. Then, something caught my eyes—a man crossing
the street entered a building with a sign that read, 'Spiritual
Healing Center.' Some magnetic force seemed to pull me
toward him, and without thinking, I followed him. He was the
director of the center, responsible for managing and
conducting spiritual readings for people. After finding out
what he does, I scheduled an appointment for the spiritual
reading later that day, hoping he might give me some guidance

in the new city.

During my spiritual reading, I shared my situation with him, then, he responded,

"Actually, we need help."

He suggested that I work at his center in exchange for food and board. It was the first time in my life I had ever considered in any kind of work trade. However, it turned out to be a perfect deal.

The Spiritual Healing Center operated as a rehab for individuals struggling with drug addiction or alcoholism. The clients who stayed there followed a structured schedule aimed at detoxifying both their bodies and minds. It included vegan meals, meditation, yoga, Tai Chi, and other healing practices. For me, it was an unexpected gift, Not only did I adapt a vegan diet, detoxifying my body and mind, but also I managed to break free from my 10-year-long habits of smoking cigarettes and drinking alcohol,

'*What a brilliant plan the universe had for me!*'

A few weeks after settling into the new lifestyle, working at the center, something strange happened.

While cleaning the front window of the center, I received phone calls from the modeling agencies in New York. Since they had not been informed of my relocation, they were reaching out for the casting calls− for the first time in a long time.

One of the phone calls was from a client who had partially booked for an upcoming photoshoot based on my photo. After that call, my mind became chaotic,

'I used to make good money in front of the camera. But what am I doing now? I am cleaning this stupid window and not getting paid for it. It sucks!' I sank into self−pity, and tears welled up. At that moment, the voice inside me shouted,

'*Don't forget why you left New York.*'

At the sound of the voice, I dropped the rag I had been using to clean the windows, and simultaneously, I set down all my thoughts and worries. At that moment, suddenly, an incredible amount of energy rose from my sacrum area and shot up quickly through my spine, reaching the top of my head. After then, I was never the same.

Alongside my work at the center, I devoted myself to meditation all day every day. I meditated wherever I could, even for five minutes. Whether, at the bus stop, sitting at an outdoor table at the coffee shop, on the top of Twin Peaks, or at the ocean beach, where I found a seat and allowed myself to be simply present.

The more I meditated, the clearer my mind became. With that clarity, I reached a new level of consciousness that I had never experienced before. As I deepened into my meditation, something unexplainable happened.

It was the day I went to a Nepalese restaurant with my boyfriend at that time and a friend. The moment I opened the door, the music playing inside resonated with me so deeply that I was immediately struck by it. I could not help myself—I turned to the waiter and asked,

"Excuse me, excuse me, what is this music?"

"It is the Tibetan Buddhist chant, *Om Mani Pad Me Hum,*" the waiter responded.

The moment the chant filled the air, it felt like the mantra awakened memories of my past lives, resonating deeply within my soul. All those unexplainable experiences from meditation led me to dive deeper into it. Then, synchronicity began to

Unfold. People I met started mentioning *Maui* more frequently than usual. After experiencing this ongoing synchronicity for several months, I felt compelled to follow the sign. So, in August 2006, I decided to travel to Maui with just a suitcase, not entirely sure of what waited for me but trusting that it was the right path.

Twin peaks in San Francisco, 2006

Photoed: Ora C

Maui

"Maui loves you! If Maui likes the newcomers, it wants to see their blood as a welcome sign."

I glanced down and noticed one of my fingers was bleeding from a small cut.

As soon as I stepped out of the Maui airport, my jaw dropped in awe of the magnificent mountain in front of me. And I could feel a magnetic energy emanating from the island. However, in my excitement, as I pushed my luggage cart through the airport, I stumbled and fell. I had not noticed it at first, but when I calmed down, I saw I was bleeding.

Later, people I met on Maui explained that it is considered a welcoming sign for newcomers. So, I accepted it as a spiritual greeting from the island.

My journey on Maui began in Haiku. The housemates I stayed with were filled with liberal-minded artists, including musicians, painters, DJs, and more. As I melted into their vibe, my mind became liberal as well. Meanwhile, I continued to meditate. The more I meditated, the more I transformed into a new instrument ready to be played by whatever notes and tunes coming from the universe's vibrations.

One day, I touched the keyboard in the house. Then, it brought back memories of playing piano in 4th grade. When I touched the keys for the first time, I instantly fell in love with it. Within a few months, I was playing at a level comparable to students who had been there for 3 or 4 years. Eventually, I could play any music by ear without needing to read the notes.

However, the academy's director did not like that I was playing at such a high level. She approached me in a fit of anger,

"You're not supposed to play this music at your level!"

Her outburst drained my motivation to continue at the academy, so I quit. When I got home, I asked my mother to buy me a piano. My mother responded,

"We don't have enough money to buy you a piano."

That was the last time, unaware of what I was missing. Reflecting on my 6-month experience, I took a deep breath and touched on the keyboard.

Suddenly, a beautiful melody began to flow through my body, and my fingers moved effortlessly across the keys, playing nonstop. As I immersed myself in the music, a woman entered the house and quietly sat on the couch. She was a friend of one of my roommates.

After nearly two hours of playing the music, I finally stopped. The woman on the couch stood up, approached me, and asked,

"Wow, that was such beautiful music! Are you a pianist?"

"No," I replied.

"What? You played such amazing music for hours. I thought you were a pianist!" she exclaimed.

I agreed with her. However, after playing it, I had no memory of the melody or how to play the piano in that manner. These kinds of incomprehensible experiences continued to occur while practicing meditation. After a short stay in the Haiku, I took on a work trade at a farm. Unfortunately, it was not a good fit for me, so I decided to leave–though I had no clear plan for what could come next. As the sun began to set, I prayed to the last minutes of the sunset,

'Please, help, where should I go tonight?'

Almost immediately after my prayer, my phone rang. It was Kelly.

"Quanyin (my name at that time), I found a place for you and me. Hurry up and come" she said.

"Really! I will be there soon." I responded, feeling a wave of relief.

I was so astonished by Kelly's call because she had no idea I had left the farm when she reached out.

'The universe listened to my prayer!

On my way to meet Kelly, I felt excited and eager to see how my path would unfold.

In Maui, Hawaii, 2006-2007

Photoed by Ora C
　　　　　Michael Axtell

Living in the Jungle

"You are a good person. You two are in," the landlady said.

Kelly and I moved to the spacious jungle property in Huelo, where we rented one of many houses on the land. The house was made of wood and featured a large open-outdoor terrace with a kitchen setup. However, there was no electricity, cell phone reception, or internet access, making the true beginning of our jungle lifestyle. Despite the absence of modern comforts, I was thrilled to have a new home for Kelly and me. The very next day, I set off on an adventure in the jungle.

First, I was drawn to a long swing hanging from a tall tree. I climbed on and enjoyed the sensation of swinging back and forth. As I moved through the air, I noticed a little black pig roaming nearby, surrounded by the dogs and cats playing together. It felt like a scene from a peaceful animated film. After getting off the swing, I continued to explore the jungle property.

The property was filled with an abundance of tropical fruit trees—bananas, coconuts, guavas, avocados, macadamia nuts, etc. I picked fresh fruit straight out of the trees and brought it back home, feeling as though I were in the Garden of Eden. As I savored the fruit, repeatedly played Stevie Wonder's song, *'Come Back As A Flower'*, which made me feel as though I was magically becoming one with nature. While I wholeheartedly enjoyed living in the jungle, one night I had an ironic experience.

When it got dark, I lit some candles. As the light from the candles spread, cockroaches nearby started to flee. Ironically, I felt sorry for frightening them rather than intimidated by their existence. Since living in the jungle, I had developed a connection with all the beings around me, and my fear of other creatures gradually faded. Meanwhile, Kelly stopped coming to the jungle house, so it became my secret sanctuary.

In the morning, I came down to a small stream that flowed through the jungle property. I found a quiet spot where no one was around. Feeling free, wild, and untouched, I jumped into the water. As I floated, the morning sunbeams filtered through the trees, casting a surreal glow over the scene, as if a fairy might appear. After emerging from the water, I sat on a large rock beside the stream and meditated for hours.

In the afternoon, I ventured to a cliff just outside the jungle property. The cliff appeared to be over 100 meters high from the bottom. I sat at the edge, which resembled a dragon's head, and began to meditate. As I meditated, a powerful wind blew through, shaking my entire body. It frightened me, and silly thoughts about being blown off the cliff. However, I managed to regain my stillness. As my meditation deepened, I experienced the most incredible moment.

I meditated just any other day. Suddenly, my body felt like an empty vessel, and then after, an abundance of light and energy poured into my body non-stop. It was a brief experience but felt like the most inconceivable energy I have ever had.

Almost a year had passed since I moved to Maui when I had a strange and unsettling dream one night. In the dream, my mother was crying in a dark, underground space. Confused, I asked her,

"Mom, why are you here?"

"I don't know..." She responded. Her voice filled with

extreme fear and sorrow.

The place she was in felt like a cold, dark hell. As soon as I woke up, I contacted her and discovered that she was suffering terribly, both physically and mentally. Until that moment, she had not fully shared her struggles with me. Realizing how ill she was, I knew I could no longer stay on Maui, despite a strong connection to the island. So, in the summer of 2007, after eight years of adventure in America, I bought a ticket to South Korea.

In the Jungle house, 2006

Photoed by Ora Cheon

2, Warrior spirit

India trip

Upon returning to South Korea after eight years, I noticed significant changes: new, numerous tall apartment complexes, more cars, digitized public systems, and pedestrians walking with their heads down, glued to their phones, and my mother's disappointment. I realized that I needed to support her financially. As a newcomer, I struggled to find work in Korea. Eventually, my circumstances led me to travel to India, where I hoped to find a guru who could help me build inner strength. *'Once I gain the strength, I will gratefully return home and help my mother,'* I thought.

So, after 3 weeks of staying in Korea, I flew to India in September 2007.

As soon as I arrived at Mumbai airport, I approached a man in a security uniform and asked him how to get to the 3-star hotel in the U.S. dollars. He immediately called a taxi for me. The cab dropped me at a hotel. After checking in, I opened the door to my room, only to be greeted by an unpleasant odor from a large black mold growing on the wall.

Despite my discomfort, I fainted right away. I was not only

shocked by the Indian way but also exhausted during three weeks of adjusting to life in a new Korea. After I woke up, I realized that coming to India as a backpacker was not a good idea.

I spent two nights in Mumbai before traveling to Pune to visit the Osho Ashram, hoping to meet the guru. However, the guru I sought did not exist there for me. Following recommendations from people in Pune, I made my way to Goa, eager to see the blue ocean. But when I arrived, I discovered it was the peak of typhoon season, and it rained non-stop day and night. I ended up stuck in a motel for 4 days. So far, this trip seemed like an unfortunate.

After spending for 4 nights in Goa, I boarded a plane to Jaipur. I stayed in Jaipur for one night before continuing to go to Agra. While asking people on the street for directions to the express bus terminal, a man approached me and offered to guide me. And after I got the ticket, he walked me to the bus. However, instead of the comfortable express bus I had expected, an old, small white van was waiting for the final passenger− me. I looked at the man and started to complain,

"I bought the ticket for the express bus!"

"This is the express bus!" He responded.

Although I was tempted to argue with him, I realized that doing so would only drain my energy and waste time—something I could not afford in this country. So, I accepted the situation and climbed into the van. The passengers were all men, sitting shoulder to shoulder. I squeezed myself in between them. Fortunately, the ride was quiet. After a 7-hour ride, we finally arrived in Agra. I stayed for one night in Agra before heading to Kolkata.

Kolkata was packed with countless mopeds, their countless noise filling the air day and night. It was more chaotic than any other city I had visited in India. I dropped my belongings and began to explore on foot. After walking for a while, I found myself standing on a surprisingly quiet street beneath an overpass. In that moment, everything around me seemed to slow down, fading into a blur of witness, except for the present moment.

The shimmering light reflected off the water splashes that dazzled my eyes and took my breath away. The water flowed steadily from the street pump to the ground. While children were joyfully running and playing on that surface, it created sparkling splashes that reflected the sun's rays. Their laughter—"Hahahaha"—filled the entire space, infusing the air with energy that resonated deeply with me, raising my frequency and reaching beyond the physical realm.

Later in the evening, I returned to that same street. The children I had seen earlier were sleeping side by side on the ground. They had no blankets, no beds—only pieces of cardboard stacked atop the cold cement street. Despite their harsh living conditions, they seemed to make the most of what little they had. I imagined that they would make another fantastic day the next day.

After Kolkata, I boarded a train to New Jalpaiguri, preparing to continue to my final destination, Darjeeling, to see Lama Galtsen the following day. Darjeeling was unlike any other place I had encountered in India—it was peace.

Lama Gyalsten, who had been leading the Tibetan Dharma Center on Maui, was visiting his ill mother in Sonada, near Darjeeling. When he saw me, his eyes widened, and his jaw dropped in surprise.

"Wow, I am amazed to see you here! Did you come here

by yourself?" he asked.

"Yes, Lama. I came to India by myself without a guide or Pre-booked hotels", I replied.

"You are so brave!" He said.

"I don't think I am brave. I just didn't know how the trip to India would turn out. But I am happy to see you!" I said.

He served me tea and cookies as I shared stories of my travels across India. Spending time with him soothed restlessness in my mind and soul after the long journey. When I left Lama, I felt a renewed sense of hope and decided to travel to London.

Lama Gyaltsen

Photoed by Ora C

Kelly

After I checked in at the YMCA near the London airport, I found a flat within a week. It was sometime in October 2007.

The flat was located on the north side of London, near Alexandra Park & Palace. Fortunately, the landlord was a nice guy. After nearly a month of staying there, my flatmates were having a picnic in the park. As the picnic was wrapping up, I opened up about my situation.

"I came to London from India, where I had spent three weeks backpacking. The reason I went to India was that I suddenly had to return to Korea this summer to take care of my ill mom after living in the U.S. for eight years. However, having been away for so long, I had no idea where to start or how to find work in Korea. So, I went to India, hoping to find a guru who could help my inner strength. But I did not meet the guru I was searching for there. On the last day of the India trip, I decided to come to London in hopes of finding some modeling opportunities, like the ones I had in New York City. But, so far, nothing has come my way... I don't think I can make it for the next month to live with you guys." I said.

"You can stay at my place if you need", Simon, a friend of one of my flatmates said,

I eventually, decided to stay at Simon's place.

In his house, I immediately felt the warm vibe. I settled onto his couch in his living room. As soon as I sat down, my restless body and mind from the India trip and struggle to find a job in London began to melt away. He lit some candles, and we talked until they burned down. When our conversation ended, he hung a curtain at the entrance of the living room to give me some privacy. I truly appreciated his warmheartedness. That night, I slept so well for the first time in a long time.

Simon was a psychotherapist at the police station, where he counseled kids who got arrested by the policemen.

The next day, when he returned home, I was meditating in his living room. I invited him to join if he wanted. After he finished, he told me it was his first time meditating. While I stayed at Simon's house, I was able to meditate either at his house or walking meditation for miles.

After almost 2 months of staying at his place, he invited me to a live concert at a local bar. During the show, a sudden wave of sadness washed over me, and I could not stay inside the bar. With my head down and lost in my thoughts, I walked slowly outside.

A bright light shooting from the ground hit my face, amplifying my emotions even more. It mixed with a deep sense of regret for leaving my mother again and enormously longing for Maui. At that moment, someone in golden sneakers approached me. I lifted my head to see who it was.

A petite, young British woman with a cigarette stood in front of me. She offered me the one she was smoking, and she said,

"Do you want this?"

Without a second thought, I took her cigarette. We locked eyes, and her gaze was intense, piercing. Then she began telling me who I am,

"You are..."

What she said completely blew my mind, and I just listened intently until she had finished delivering her entire message. Then, she walked away. The only thing I knew about her was her name, Kelly.

After meeting her, something inside me shifted, and I felt a deep connection to the warrior spirit. Eventually, I ended my three-month London trip in December 2007 and returned to Korea to care for my mother.

A twin angel statue

Photoed by Ora C

No more addiction

On a massive snowy day in the winter of 2004, my father went for a bike ride. Unfortunately, a tragedy occurred. He fell off his bike and collided with a rock hidden beneath the snow on the street. The impact was so severe that fractured his hip bone. The worst part was that he slipped into a coma after the accident.

The doctor informed my family that he would not live for more than a month. Following the diagnosis, my mother decided to bring him home and care for him until the end of his life. Surprisingly, he lived far longer than the doctor's prediction—an additional one and a half years in a coma. It seemed that my mother's care and devotion had given him a chance to hold.

My mother began diligently cleaning his wounds with alcohol twice a day before she went to work and again after she returned. She also took care of his feeding and daily hygiene needs, including his excretions. Despite her best efforts, his body continued to emit a rotting odor, which worsened over time. I found all of this after returning to Korea in 2007. I felt deeply terrible that I was not there to help my mother during her challenging time.

After my father passed away, my mother's grief was frequently triggered by the memory of his death. She burst into tears almost every ten minutes, haunted by those memories. I had to constantly comfort her and said,

"Mom, it's over. The past no longer exists. Look! I am here. I came here for you. Please, eat. I cooked it for you,"

She would smile briefly, but her mind would quickly return to the past and shed her tears again.

It has been a month since I returned home. I saw her crying again. At that moment, I lost control and yelled at her in frustration,

"Mom! How many times do I have to tell you to stop crying? Stop dwelling in the past! The past does not exist anymore! I came back here for you, but you don't even know how I feel. Please, stop crying!"

"How dare you yell at me, to your mom?" My mother immediately yelled back at me.

She walked into her room, slammed the door behind her, and cried even harder. At that time, my heart was deeply hurt for causing her pain. I cried as hard as she did behind the closed door: '*I came here to heal her, not hurt her.*'

After about 30 minutes, she paused her crying and remained silent for a while. She then opened the door, walked out of her room, and said,

"You are right. What you said is right."

Since then, my mother's mind began to focus on the present moment, and she cried less frequently. Meanwhile, I taught her Kouk Sun Do, which helped her regain physical strength as well as Hangul (the Korean language), which she could learn to read and write. Unfortunately, when my mother was little, she did not have an opportunity to attend school.

My mother was approximately 7 or 8 years old girl when the Korean War ended in 1953. Her parents had little money left after the war. They could afford to send their sons not daughters to school. Instead of attending school, my mom began working at the age of nine. by 13, she left home to earn money. She worked in textile factories, moved to restaurants, and took on other physically demanding jobs. Over time, she managed her money wisely and was able to buy some land in her hometown for her parents, which they began farming on the land. She also helped her three brothers pay their high school tuition. I remember her money-saving strategies. When our family ordered some food, she always said she was not hungry.

It had been a year and a half since I began caring for my mother. After returning home from my job, teaching English at an academy, I opened the door to my mother's apartment, and heard her voice. She was reading a book while laughing. I quietly opened her room and said,

"Mom, I am home."

"Oori Aegi Jibewasseo! Omma Haengboghada ('My baby, you are home! I am so happy' in Korean)", she said and looked at me with shining eyes and said.

I smiled at her and closed the door gently. Behind that

closed door, I raised my arms in triumph,

'Yes! I did it! I healed my mother. My mission is completed!'.

During the two years I spent caring for my mother, I was able to strengthen my energy through natural celibacy. This practice helped me to break free from all addictions, including alcohol and cigarettes. I also concentrated on personal development by practicing Zen meditation, Kouk Sun Do, traditional Chinese medicine, and learning Taoism.

Meanwhile, my mother healed, her intuition returned. One day she said to me,

"You want to go back to America, don't you? Go, if you want to. I am fine now."

After my father passed away, she was so afraid of living alone. On the first day of my return to Korea, she begged me not to leave her. Interestingly, after she allowed me, synchronicity came to me. The man I had a 2-year long-distance relationship with, who lived in the United States proposed to me. So, I flew back to the U.S. at the end of 2009. However, the universe had another plan for me.

A mural at The women's building in San Francisco

Photoed by Ora C

Part 3,

Ora: Come to me

'No problem can be solved from the same level of consciousness'.

-Einstein-

1, Now

Mermaid

A gold shimmering band appeared just above the ocean as the sun dipped below the horizon. This scene emerged at Venice Beach in L.A. in December 2017.

I brushed the sand off my hips and began to walk down a street parallel to the beach. I noticed that the street vendors and performers were wrapping up for the day. After walking for a while, I suddenly stopped, struck by what I saw.

"Am I tripping?" I said inside.

In front of me stood a beautiful and sensual piece of art, seemingly inhabited by a spirit. I approached a woman standing behind it.

"Are you the artist who made this? I asked.

"Yes," she replied.

"Do you swipe it away before you go home?" I asked.

"Yes," she answered.

"How long does it take to complete?" I asked her again.

"All day. I just finished it. I will show people for a few hours, then swipe it away before I go home," she said.

"Wow! What you are doing is like the Tibetan monastic practice! The monks spend days and months creating a beautiful, colorful mandala, only to swipe them away shortly after completion. This practice symbolizes, *'Impermanence'*. It helps cultivate non-attachment to the things we work hard for. When we leave our physical bodies, we cannot take our possessions with us. By accepting impermanence, we can transcend the physical realm when the time comes. It seems like you truly understand this." I spoked.

"Yes, it is only now that matters. There is no past or future: only this present moment is truly real. The past exists as memory, and the future is uncertain. Only the now is real." She spoke.

The artist was Mary Klein, the creator of the ground-based sand mermaid statue.

After meeting her, I felt a sense of relief from my four-month relationship. Then, the ocean breeze felt refreshing.

Everything is constantly changing, and that makes the present moment more beautiful and appreciated.

On Venice beach street in California, 2018

Photoed by Ora C

Forgiveness heals the wounded heart

        I was on a bus traveling down on Sunset
Boulevard. In the middle of riding, suddenly, an unknown,
powerful force pierced my heart, causing me to cry. No matter
how hard I tried to stop, I could not. It was not until an hour
later, when I finally got off the bus, that tears stopped. This
was one of the most inexplicable experiences since I started
meditating. This strange experience took place in Los Angeles
sometime in August 2017.

    Soon after an hour of uncontrollable tears, a vivid vision
suddenly appeared to me. In the vision, there was a man, a
child who looked like 4 or 5 years old, and me. The man in
the vision was someone I had known as an acquaintance for a
few years. I shook my head dismissing my thought, 'No, no,
no...'

    A month later, the same image appeared to me again. By
then, I had come to believe that the man in the picture would
one day become the father of my future child– the 4 or 5–
year–old in the picture – and that we would start a family
together. Based on my interpretation, I decided to meet him.

However, once we began seeing each other, I was deeply hurt. After enduring pain for a while, I asked him to set a time for a conversation.

"My fear drove that." He said.

During our conversation, he realized that, due to his past experience, he had unconsciously closed his heart. With his closed heart, there was no real connection between us. It was the first time I truly understood how painful it could be to be in a relationship without a true emotional bond.

Four months later, I finally had a serious conversation with him about the vision I had seen. In response, he said,

"That's your picture, not mine. If you want to have a baby with me, I will consider you to become a single mom."

Soon after his statement, I realized that I misinterpreted the vision, which led me end my relationship with him.

While going through the confusion and dramatic time, I committed to praying for an hour every day for a month, using the Kwanseum Bosal Kido (Mantra). After a month of prayer, a sense of forgiveness emerged in my heart.

I forgave myself for misinterpreting the image and acting impatiently based on my mistaken belief. Once I forgave myself, the uneasy feelings I had toward him cleared, and compassion began to fill in my heart. With that compassion, I prayed for him,

'Please, help him to overcome his fear and open his heart'.

Eight months after our breakup, I heard he had married someone.

As time passed, I shared this strange experience with someone I knew, and he said,

"In your picture, the man you had seen for 4 months would cause you great pain. So, while overcoming your suffering, you evolved into a new version of yourself. And the 4 or 5-year-old child in your picture would symbolize Trinity, representing the new version, is you."

Forgiveness is the act of releasing the heavy emotions from the past that you have been holding onto. When you let go of these burdens, you will feel clearer, lighter, and be healed. With this shift in mindset, you will align yourself with a new frequency— the higher frequency. As you tune into this elevated vibration, you will begin to attract people who resonate with it and encounter circumstances that align with your new energy.

   -In Taoist philosophy, the harmony of yin and yang represents the balance between feminine and masculine energies. To achieve harmony in our life between these polarities, we need to recognize that it is essential to be altruistic, less selfish, show respect, and care for each other-

At Venice in California in 2017

Photoed by Ora C

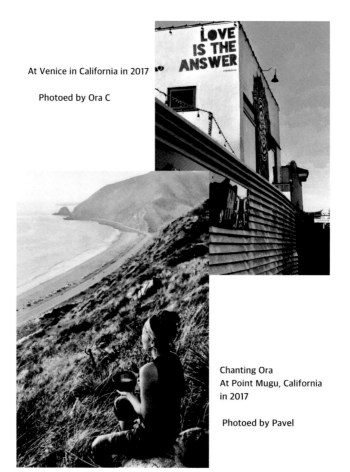

Chanting Ora
At Point Mugu, California
in 2017

Photoed by Pavel

Kiss

The sky transformed into a magic pink as if it were set up for a lovely couple. As the groom and the bride held each other's hands and united, tears began to fall from their eyes. I, too, resonated with the depth of their love, and tears flew from my eyes. It was a small wedding held on a private property next to Lahaina Beach in Maui, Hawaii, in 2006.

At Lahaina, Maui, Hawaii

Photoed by Ora C

Once the ceremony ended, everyone gathered to eat and drink. However, I walked away from the crowd to get some fresh air.

A few stars had already appeared, competing for brightness. As I walked, the dazzling light from the bottom of the pool in the yard caught my eye, tempting me to dive in. I took my clothes off and plunged into the water. My body moved freely as if I were part of the watery dimension, and my mind dissolved into tranquility. After refreshing myself, I sat by the pool and gazed up at the night sky.

Thousands of stars twinkled above as if they were telling me a story. It was a breathtaking moment. While fully engaged in the moment, suddenly, I felt a strong, energetic vibe from a distance. I turned my head to see where the sensation came from.

A blonde boy in the distance was walking toward me. He then stopped in front of me and gently sat down beside me. I recognized him as one of three young boy surfers with surfboards who walked into the wedding ceremony area by accident. Nevertheless, the groom and the bride welcomed them.

"Hi," he said.

"Hi," I replied.

After I said, *Hi*, we remained silent for a minute. Then he started talking to me again.

"You look familiar! Oh, I remember you! Do you remember me? I worked as a cashier at the food corner on Front Street. We met a couple of weeks ago. Remember me?"

"Oh, that's right!" I remembered as I looked at him closely.

"Wow, I can't believe this. Right after you walked away, I felt I would see you again. But I didn't expect it to be so soon." He said.

"Really?" I smiled at what he said.

In that instant, our eyes met. He came closer to me, and his lips lightly touched mine. I pulled myself back in shock, but my resistance melted away. We then started kissing, and it seemed to become infinite, like Mikey ways in space.
Lost in that moment, I unconsciously opened my eyes, and then, a long-tailed shooting star I caught, '*Magic!*'.

Time seemed to stop. We slowly stood up and walked toward the beach. Even the crashing waves could not stop us. Then, suddenly,

"What? Did you hear that?" He asked, his voice filled with surprise.

"Oh my god!" I responded, equally shocked.

"That's crazy!" He said.

We finally broke our kiss, startled by a strange noise. To our surprise, we had unintentionally made a high-pitched bird-chirping sound with our mouths. We exchanged a look at each other and burst out laughing like children,

"Hahahaha⋯"

Life is not always logical. The magical and mysterious moments I experienced might have been created by a pure heart, being fully present, 'now', and staying relaxed.

A shooting star

Photoed by O-Chul Kwon

2, High frequency

Natural Healing

Most WWOOFers at the farm in Maui, Hawaii, where I worked, had recently graduated high school. They joined the program to explore their options before deciding whether to attend college. Others were in their 20s and seasoned world travelers. The WWOOF (The World Wide Opportunities on Organic Farms) program involves exchanging work for room and board on organic farms. I took this program on and off from 2013 to 2015.

After 5 hours of farming in the morning, we either went swimming in the ocean or visited the waterfall together. Sometimes, we ventured through the lush Maui jungle on a hike.

In the evening, we gathered in a lounge room and relaxed. Some played chess or other games, while others played the guitar until midnight. Occasionally, we had a special night with a campfire on the farm.

The smell of burning wood and watching the dancing flames beneath the thousands of stars tripped me beyond the physical dimension, where there was no worry.

On the left, a wwoofer
& Ora,
and the middel, left, &
the right top are WWOOFers

At Dragon fruit Fram & Greenleaf from 2013 to 2015
In Maui, Hawaii

Touching the earth through farming grounded me in the embrace of Āina (land). Additionally, practicing yoga and meditation in nature healed my mind, heart, and spirit after my divorce. Recharging my energy and restoring balance also helped to raise my frequency. The deep connection to nature began in my early childhood.

Most modern-day children have toys, video games, cell phones, and computers, spending most of their time playing indoors. However, when I was a little girl, I was not given man-made products. Instead, I found infinite joy in nature as soon as I learned to walk as a little girl.

In the spring, the light green rice seedlings were just transplanted into the field. By the early summer, around June, the typhoon would bring heavy rain before the heat of the summer arrived. After the long, rainy season, the rice plants grew taller than me, I was as three or four years old and turned vibrant green. My neighborhood friends and I ran barefoot down the dirt path, lost in the endless green world. We spent hours observing the water creatures in the field, watching until sunset. And my favorite rice field appeared in the fall.

In the fall, the entire rice field turned a vivid yellow, and a clear blue sky stretched above. Countless dragonflies flitted between these contrasting colors, and as I followed them, I felt as if I had wandered into the page of a fairy tale.

During the harvest season, the rice plants were cut down, and the stalks were piled into large haystacks. One of the haystacks was carved out to create a hollow the size of a large room. My friend and I would hide inside, the warmth of the hay wrapping around as we ate radishes from leftovers in the field. Then, as winter arrived, the entire world transformed into a magic white realm by snow.

After the snow fell, the rice fields froze, turning into icy. My friends and I brought our sleighs and spent the entire day sledding and laughing, having the timeless joy of the moment.

Growing up and walking barefoot in nature, I naturally connected with the Earth's energy, known as *Ji Ki* in Korean. Through meditation, I also learned to connect with *Cheon Ki*, the energy of the universe. By balancing these energies within my body, I believe I can raise my frequency and unblock my limitless imagination.

Home, Korea

Photoed by Ora C

I am Nailed

A man in a black sleeveless top just ran past me. I immediately felt his strong energy and turned to see where he was heading. Then, I noticed his shirt—there was a large white "X" on the front and a phrase, "I am Nailed" on the back. Driven by my curiosity, I called out to him just as he was about to enter his apartment,

"Excuse me."

He turned back to face me. *'Wow!'* His eyes radiated a bright light that took my breath away for a moment. When my mind returned to the present moment, I asked him,

"What does that mean? I am Nailed on your shirt."

"Oh, I have not drunk, smoked, or used any other drug since college. I used to do all of that stuff during my college years, but I quit, and I have been sobered for 20 years.

I am now 40 years old and run 10 miles a day, every day. Living soberly has made my life successful, and I now run my own business here in Los Angeles and Switzerland. 'X' means 'No' which means I am nailed not to use those substances." he replied.

It was on my way to hike to Runyon Canyon in Los Angeles in the summer of 2017.

Encountering him reminded me of something Lama Gyaltsen said to me one day:

"True consciousness develops in a sober state, without the influence of drugs or alcohol, or any substance."

At Los Angeles in 2017

Photoed by Ora C

Miyeokguk

Jax, a 7-month-old boy tightly gripped my pinkie with his left hand after I said "Hi" to him, and he refused to let go. While he held onto my little finger, I spoke to Shelby, Jax's mother.,

"I can feel Jax's *Ki* (energy). It is so strong and calm."

"Jax is stronger than my 7-year-old twins. Throughout my pregnancy with him, my body naturally craved fresh food rather than processed or fast foods. The most I have eaten was Miyeokguk (a seaweed soup)" Shelby responded.

"Miyeokguk? Really? That is a Korean traditional dish! Miyeok (seaweed) is known to detoxify blood in the body. That's why, according to Korean tradition, women eat it after giving birth to help reduce swelling. And Koreans also eat it on their birthdays. I think it means to honor their mothers who ate it during childbirth," I said.

"We eat Myeokguk once a week. Sometimes, we add meat or noodles to it. And we also love to eat kimchi and bone soup," Shelby's husband said. He is Italian American.

"That's a surprise! You two eat Korean food more frequently than I do, even though you are American! And kimchi and bone soup too? Kimchi is known as the best probiotic for digestion—it contains beneficial bacteria that fight against harmful bacteria in our bodies". I enthusiastically explained, sharing my love for Korean food and telling her about my favorite Korean dishes.

"One of my favorite Korean food is Ssuck dduck (mugwort rice cake) and Ssuck doenjangkuk (mugwort misso soup). My mom used to cook for me when I was a little girl" I said.

Mugwort is known as an herb for liver detoxication, its ability to enhance immunity, and acts as an anti-cancer agent.

Shelby, whom I met at Thanksgiving dinner at my friend's house on November 24th, is 31 years old and originally from Philadelphia. She left her hometown at the age of 16. Since then, she has lived in various places and met many people, gaining wisdom on how to live her life. One of her Korean

American friends introduced her to Miyeokguk.

We maintain different levels of energy depending on the food we consume. As a result, conscious eating habits are essential for preventing both physical and mental health. A healthy body and mind can also help elevate your frequency.

On Thanksgiving in 2022
with Shelby, her family, and other friends in Maui, Hawaii

Photoed by Ora C

Holy Fish

As we paddled further into the ocean, the waves grew bigger and rougher, causing the canoe to rise and fall more vigorously. Even though I was not a strong swimmer, I felt a thrilling excitement as if I were an adventurous movie rather than fear.

2, to 3 miles after we began paddling, the captain called out, 'Lava (which means "Finish" in Hawaiian).' We stopped and set down our paddles. As the canoe filled halfway with water from the rough waves, we began to scoop it out using a half-gallon bottle. Once the canoe was dry, I gazed out at the vast, deep blue ocean. Mesmerized by the beauty of Mother Nature, I lost myself in the moment until something suddenly happened in front of me.

A massive black shape suddenly emerged from the ocean right in front of the canoe. It expelled a spray of water before quickly disappearing back beneath the surface. Everyone on the canoe shouted, "Whale!" but I was so stunned that I could not speak; my jaw just dropped. The captain of the canoe called out something in Hawaiian, and everyone raised their paddles straight up in a gesture of respect and honor to the whale. I did the same, following the others.

In that moment, I deeply appreciated the incredible, sacred presence of the whale, feeling the holiness of the encounter. Since then, my frequency increased significantly and stayed elevated for quite some time. It was early Sunday morning in April 2021 at the canoe club in Maui, Hawaii, only my second time canoeing.

If we humans lived less selfishly and greedily and instead connected more with nature—living in harmony with it— we could experience the limitless resources and spontaneous joy that nature offers, simply because we coexist with it.

Ora in Maui, Hawaii, 2021

Photoed by Scott Corderman

3, Ora: Come to me

Ora: Come to me

The word, Ora means in Korean, 'Come to me'

An elderly lady wearing a traditional Korean white dress was wrapped around a tree branch with her arms. I noticed her down the trail back from Hwaeomsa, the Buddhist temple in Jirisan (Jiri Mountain). It was the summer of 2008 in South Korea. I approached her and asked if she was all right,

"Harmoni, (means 'Grandma' in Korean as an informal way to call the elderly woman), are you okay?" I asked.

"Ya, I am fine." She responded.

"Can I help you?" I asked her again if she needed any assistance.

"No, I am just taking a break from walking down the trail. I was on my way from Hwaeomsa. When I go to Hwaeomsa, I take a taxi, but the return trip is downhill, so I walk." She said.

"Oh, I see," I replied.

After checking with her, I continued down the trail, and she began walking alongside me. As we walked together, we initiated a conversation. As our conversation was coming to an end, she stated,

"You are a young woman but you have already been awakened. When is your birthday?"

After I informed her of my birthday, she gathered her thoughts and said,

"Young woman, you will reap what you have sown after you turn forty. It will all come to you."

"It will all **come to me**?" I responded.

Selfie, a reflection of me on a side mirror

Photoed by Ora C

Experience

      We humans unconsciously and consciously, influence each other as we go through life.

My own journey has been shaped by encounters with countless and diverse people. Those with open minds‑ whether women, men, children, the elderly, or individuals of any background‑ enriched my existence through communication, connection, appreciation, caring, sharing, and mutual inspiration. Now, in 2024, the world is transitioning from direct human relationships to interactions with AI. So then, how will humanity change in this new era?

Even if we can achieve infinite awakening in an ever‑ changing world, this life will pass quickly like a shooting star. That is why being in the present moment is such a present.

−The mystical experience Satori, the realization that you are the eternal energy of the universe. You cannot catch hold of it, nor can you get rid of it, in not being able to get it, you get it. When you speak, it's silent. When you are silent, it speaks.

Now, in not being able to get, get it, because there is no method. All methods simply gimmick for strengthening your ego−

Ora, and people who were in Ora's journeys

The Owl

       Driving on a rainy night with no streetlights was quite challenging for me, especially as a beginner driver.

I had just dropped off my friend's friend in Paia and continued to drive down Baldwin Avenue. As I approached a turn, I saw headlights in the distance. My mind said, *'Let the car go'*, but my foot pressed the gas pedal to accelerate instead.

Soon, the car behind me honked and tailgated me—as the saying goes, "*Ride my ass.*" It was a tense moment as I was driving on a winding road under the weather currency. While I was looking for the spot to pull over and yield to the car, suddenly, large white wings appeared and vanished as quickly as they had appeared, *'Am I hallucinating because of the weather?'* But I was not. I had to stop the car immediately for the bird that was sitting on the middle of the road.

Normally, birds on the road fly away when a vehicle approaches. However, it remained in place.

It appeared to be a young adult white, its round head standing sideway with its head turned toward me. When its black eyes met mine, time seemed to pause. I lost my sense of reality. When my mind finally returned, I said,

"Oh, My, God! It's the owl. It's Owl!"

Everyone in the car was asleep except Christian who was sitting behind me. He moved closer, leaned in, and whispered in my ear,

"Oh, my God! Ora, the owl found you!"

It happened on a night in October 2018 in Maui, Hawaii, while driving back to Makawao from Lahaina.

In Hawaiian mythology, the owl is a magical bird symbolizing an extraordinary guide for the soul. It is renowned for its intuition, the ability to perceive what others cannot.

'Why did the owl come to find me that night?'

The moment marked the beginning of something greater, and the journey, it started continuing and unfolding even today.

'Owl spirit' photo art
Artist: Ora C

Owl sculpture in Maui, Hawaii
Artist: William

A Mother's Hand is a Healing Hand

발 행	Published	2023년 12월 23일/ 12.23. 2023
저 자	Author	Ora Cheon Instagram @orahealer
		Email:ora.come2me@gmail.com
편 집	Editor	Ora Cheon
사진 편집	Photo design	Ora Cheon
표지 디자인	Cover design	enBergen enbergen3@gmail.com
펴 낸 이	CEO of Publisher	한건희
펴 낸 곳	Publisher	BOOKK Co.,Ltd
출판사 등록	Date of Established Publisher: 07. 15. 2014 (제 2014-16호)
주 소	address of Publisher: 119 Gasan digital 1-ro Geumcheon-gu
	Seoul, Republic of Korea (08589)
	서울특별시 금천구 가산디지털 1로 119
	SK 트윈타워 A동 305호
전 화	Phone	1670-8361
이 메 일	Email	info@bookk.co.kr

ISBN   979-11-410-6201-9

www.bookk.co.kr